A Study G...... ...

Reading and Understanding
at Key Stage 3

Levels 4-7

By Janet Marsh

V1.0

INTRODUCTION

The material contained in this book is meant to supplement and enhance learning at Key Stage 3. The exercises and tasks will enable teachers of English to offer practice in reading, writing, speaking and listening skills. In addition, there will be opportunities to access background information where appropriate to enhance understanding and appreciation of texts.

Every effort is made to ensure that the information provided in this publication is accurate. It is the policy of Coleridge Press to obtain permission on any copyright material in their publications. The publishers will be glad to make suitable arrangements with any copyright holders whom it has not been possible to contact.

Purchasers may photocopy the sheets in this book provided that they do so only for use within their own institution.

ISBN 978-0-993273-50-6

Text by: Janet Marsh
Design and Layout by: David Jones

Pu~~blished by Coleridge P~~ess

Cop~~yright © Coleridge Press~~ 2015

Contents
Section A - Fiction

Section B – Non-Fiction

A Study Guide to...

Reading and Understanding
at Key Stage 3

WHEN WE READ A PIECE OF TEXT- IN A BOOK, IN A LEAFLET, ON THE WEB - WE USE A NUMBER OF DIFFERENT READING TECHNIQUES:-

SKIM - which means reading over the surface of the text to select the details we want.   We don't read every word, just get the main points.   To help us pick out the main points we can look at:-   o   NAMES, of people and places so that we know who is doing what – and where.   o   ACTIONS which will help us follow a story or the plot.   o   The first sentence of each paragraph which should sum up what the paragraph is going to be about.   o   Any keyword that we may be searching for to find the information we are reading.
SCAN - picking out information.   It means reading very quickly, having an eye out for key information.
INFERENCE / CLOSE READING - with close attention to the words used and drawing conclusions from the WAY the words are written.

SKIMMING AND SCANNING - are low level skills compared to **INFERENCE** and when you do comprehension tests/exams, this is reflected in the marks awarded.

Section A

Fiction

PROSE

Now SKIM AND SCAN the following piece from a novel to get the main idea of what is going on:

A

SNOWED IN

Back in school in January, the weather had turned much colder and there were even three days when school was closed due to heavy snow and virtually impassable roads.   Matthew and Nick made a sledge out of plastic milk crates with Nadeem and Saima and they spent the whole afternoon messing around on it, trying to devise ways of making it go faster and arguing about whose turn it was to have the next go.

They went back to Matthew's house to thaw out and to put their soaking wet gloves and hats on the radiators while Matthew made them all hot drinks.   They had the run of the house as Mum was in work and Lucy was "studying" at Greg's.   No matter how much time Tony was spending at theirs he showed no signs of moving in and that was how Matthew and Lucy hoped it would stay.

"I don't really want to go out again, do you?" asked Nadeem to no one in particular as he sipped his hot chocolate, his feet bare and curled up underneath him in the chair while his socks dried off on the radiator.   "It's nice here – and it'll be dark soon anyway.   What time'll your mum be home?"

"Not till half five today.   Stay if you like.   I've had enough ice and snow today.   I could get my games machine down from my bedroom and we could set it up on the big tele."

ANSWER THE FOLLOWING:-

1. How long was the school shut for during the cold weather?

2. How many of the children were sledging?   What were their names?

3. What does the extract tell us they were wearing to keep out the cold?   Quote the sentence that tells us this.

4. Who made everyone hot drinks?

Now spotting those answers wasn't too difficult, but there is more to the extract than just those facts and for us to get more out of it, we have to read more carefully, READ BETWEEN THE LINES.   To do this, we have to use the skills of DEDUCTION AND INFERENCE.

For example, if you read:

'Jack sighed, looked at his watch for the tenth time and tapped his foot impatiently.'

What would you deduce about Jack's mood?

• That he was excited?

• That he was scared?

• That he was bored?

Clearly the third option because these are actions you associate with boredom - but the writer has not SAID..............................**Jack was bored.**

He has done what good writers do:

SHOWN NOT TOLD.

From Jack's behaviour we infer / deduce that Jack was bored.

SECTION A – Fiction | *Prose*

Shown Not Told

Now try this.

> Jamal's hands shook as he held the rope. He thought his sweating
> fingers might slide and lose their grip at any moment. His body
> seemed to be swinging out of control, but the instructor was shouting
> words of encouragement. The rock face loomed above him,
> terrifyingly steep, but Neil and the others appeared to be clawing
> their way up steadily and he could even hear short bursts of laughter
> on the breeze.

1. What can you infer from this extract about Jamal's mood? Quote words and phrases as evidence.
2. How can we tell he's got plenty of support?
3. What can we tell about the attitude of Neil and the others?
4. What you have done here is to READ CLOSELY and search for clues:-

- *His hands shook*
- *His fingers sweated*
- *His body seemed out of control*
- *The rock face loomed and was terrifyingly steep.*

NOW GO BACK TO PASSAGE ⟨A⟩ AND TRY TO ANSWER THESE QUESTIONS THAT TEST YOUR POWERS OF DEDUCTION:-

1. How do we know it was difficult for people to travel around during this winter weather? Quote the phrase that tells us.
2. Why does the passage say that Lucy was "studying" at Greg's? Why are the inverted commas used here?
3. Quote the phrase that show us that Matthew and Lucy are not anxious for Tony to move in. Who do you think Tony might be?

Obviously when you are reading it is helpful to know as many words as possible, but you can often make a guess at an unfamiliar word if it's in CONTEXT (look at the words around it, think about what the writing is about).

Try these:-

1. The poor boy was struggling to read the words in the book as he was **illiterate.**

2. I can't accept your excuse for being late as it's totally **incredible.**

3. From the **summit** of the mountain you could see four different counties.

4. To remind him of his trip to Barcelona he bought his daughter a **souvenir.**

5. He **reacted** badly to the injection and developed an itchy rash.

Sometimes you can come across a word that is similar to another word you DO recognise e.g. IMPASSABLE.

You know PASS, you may know that putting IM at the front of a words (a prefix) can make a word the OPPOSITE so IMPASSABLE= cannot be passed = closed = shut by ice and snow. Don't give up on unfamiliar words.   They can often be broken down or guessed intelligently.

Try these:-

- ILLOGICAL   _____
- DISLOYAL   _____
- IMMATURE   _____
- INCAPABLE   _____
- ILLEGIBLE   _____

What do you think the underlined words in the following extract from a story mean?

Will's explanation for the key's disappearance was a completely plausible excuse. He was always stealing things. He didn't seem to be able to help himself - he was legendary in Year 8. Only last week he'd acquired a brand new parka after a visit to the Sports Centre and when interrogated by his mother, he claimed he couldn't remember picking it up. Will assumed that the keys were now in his possession, having been picked up casually by him, innocently, meaning no harm, but just like a jackdaw or magpie, simply because they were bright and shiny. The problem of how to extricate them from his pockets remained; the more interest you showed in what he'd got, the more uncooperative Seth became. He'd deny it, she knew he would. Far better to bide her time and wait until the next glittering object fascinated him enough to make him neglect the keys. Will resolved to be patient and watch for the first opportunity to reclaim the keys.

RYAN AND MR DODDS

By the end of September Ryan was in trouble. Not that that was anything new but this was serious stuff.

Most of his teachers knew his name within the first week of term, never a good sign. By the end of the first fortnight he had accumulated sixteen demerits and was called in to see Mr Dodd's his Head of Year.

Ryan had made the concession of dumping his chewing gum and he'd taken out his earring. He'd even tucked his shirt in to his trousers so as not to get off to a bad start. Teachers went off on one if you didn't at least pretend to be obeying the rules. What he couldn't remove, however, was the expression, a mixture of defiance and contempt which made every teacher's hackles rise.

SECTION A – Fiction

Mr Dodds was dealing with another offender when Ryan knocked on his door.

"Wait!" shouted a very rattled Mr Dodds.   Moments later a girl with a wet face and an angry expression flung out of the office and pushed past Ryan.

"Sit down, Ryan," instructed Mr Dodds without looking up from the forms on his desk as Ryan hovered in the doorway.

"Planner," he demanded and he held out his hand.

All St Edward's pupils were issued with these personal planners in which they recorded homework set, test dates and which provided an ongoing record of their merits for good work and behaviour, or, as in Ryan's case, demerits for missing homework and for bad behaviour.   Ryan rummaged in his school bag and produced his planner, dog eared and graffitied after only two weeks of school. Mr Dodds looked from it to its owner and raised his eyebrows with a weary sigh.   He read through the teachers' comments and sighed again, finally throwing the planner in disgust onto his desk, removing his steel framed glasses and rubbing the bridge of his nose.

"Two weeks! Two weeks in school and you've shown yourself to be disruptive, lazy and uncooperative."   He got up and walked around his desk.   Ryan tried to look contrite but it wasn't successful.   His face just wouldn't respond.   Instead it looked sneering and unpleasant.

"You are not going to be allowed to continue like this.   You will toe the line and follow the standards we have set down in this school.   You will NOT be allowed to disrupt the education of other pupils or be rude to your teachers.   DO YOU UNDERSTAND ME?" and he bellowed in Ryan's ear, causing him to blink and jump.

"No sir - I mean yes sir."

SECTION A – Fiction | Prose

extract RYAN AND MR DODDS

"Why do you do it, Ryan? Mr Dodds' voice had become softer now and he <u>perched</u> on the edge of his desk opposite Ryan. Ryan recognised the technique of "nice cop, nasty cop", played quite cleverly, he thought, by just one person. Ryan had seen it played for real from the age of eight when he'd had his first brush with the law.

"Dunno, sir," his voice now became sulky and he looked down at his ink stained and grubby fingers. There was a long silence in which a bell rang shrilly and noises in the corridor outside grew gradually louder.

"Don't you like it here? What's the problem? Aren't you keeping up with the work?" Silence.

"Any problems at home you want to tell me about?" Silence.

"I want to understand why you deliberately choose to <u>flout</u> our rules and get yourself into trouble. Fancy yourself as a hard man, do you?" Mr Dodds had moved in really close now, his nose inches away from Ryan's face.

"No sir," he mumbled.

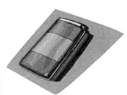 "Well," said Mr Dodds straightening up and writing in the planner, "I have no <u>alternative</u> but to give you nightly detention until your behaviour improves." He thrust the planner back at Ryan.

"We'll review the situation after two weeks of detentions. And don't think you can skive off these detentions. For everyone you miss, you get another three. Understand? Now get out of my sight!"

"Yes, sir," mumbled Ryan who <u>slouched</u> to the door and **was outside in the corridor wondering who would look after his mother from four to five while he did his detention.**

---

1. NOW HIGHLIGHT WORDS AND PHRASES THAT SHOW THE FOLLOWING:-

- how many demerits Ryan got in the first fortnight of term
- what 3 things he did before he entered the Head of Year's office
- what Ryan's planner looked like
- how we know Mr Dodds is tired / stressed / fed up with dealing with pupils like Ryan
- how we know that Ryan has been in trouble with the police
- what Ryan's punishment will be.

2. What do you think the underlined words mean?   Remember if you don't know, look at the context and try to work it out.

3. Now look at the last sentence of the extract in bold.   Here we are given a clue about Ryan's home life.   What do you think it might be hinting at?

Now you are ready to write the answers fully, using the PEE method.

| P | stands for the point you are making

| E | stands for the evidence you are using to prove your point

| E | is for the explanation you are giving

To show how this technique works, look at this short extract from Louis Sachar's novel Holes:

There is no lake at Camp Green Lake.   There was once a very large lake there, the largest lake in Texas.   That was over a hundred years ago.   Now it is just a dry, flat wasteland.

There used to be a town of Green Lake as well.   The town shrivelled and dried up along with the lake and all the people who lived there.

During the summer the daytime temperature hovers around ninety-five degrees in the shade - if you can find any shade.   There's not much shade in a big, dry lake.

The only trees are the two old oaks on the eastern edge of the 'lake'.   A hammock is stretched between the two trees and a log cabin stands behind that.

The campers are forbidden to lie in the hammock. It belongs to the Warden. The Warden owns the shade.

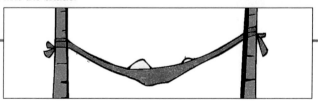

Question 1

How do we know there isn't actually a lake at Camp Green Lake?

POINTS

- we know the lake that used to be there has dried up
- the word 'lake' is placed in inverted commas to suggest it really isn't a lake.

EVIDENCE

- there 'was once' a large lake there
- it's now 'a dry flat wasteland'.

EXPLANATION

The lake dried up a hundred years ago but the name remains.

Question 2

How do we know what the summer weather is like?

POINT

It is extremely hot.

EVIDENCE

- daytime temperatures hover around ninety-five in the shade.
- if you can find any shade.
- there's not much shade in a big dry lake.
- there are only two old oak trees which give little shade.

EXPLANATION

The high temperatures and lack of trees make the whole area dry and barren.

Question 3

How does the writer suggest that Camp Green Lake is an unpleasant place to be?

POINT

- Camp Green Lake sounds hot, barren with very few people living there.

EVIDENCE

- dry flat wasteland

- the town shrivelled.....and all the people who lived there

- there's not much shade

- the only trees

- the campers are 'forbidden'

- the Warden 'owns' the shade.

EXPLANATION

Not only does the writer suggest the dry barren landscape but the lack of people, apart from the Warden who seems to have complete control of the place, suggesting it is more like a prison than anything else.

NOW USE THE P E E **METHOD TO ANSWER THE QUESTIONS ON THE FOLLOWING EXTRACTS.**

1. The following is from Michael Morpurgo's novel ***Private Peaceful***. Tommo is a young man at the outbreak of World War One. In his home town he sees a troop of soldiers and their sergeant who is recruiting men to enlist to fight in the war in France.

As I came round the corner I saw them. Behind the band there must have been a couple of dozen soldiers, splendid in their scarlet uniforms. They marched past me, arms swinging in perfect time, buttons and boots shining, the sun glinting on their bayonets. They were singing along with the band: *It's a long way to Tipperary, it's a long way to go.* Children were stomping alongside them, some wearing paper hats, some with wooden sticks over their shoulders. And there were women throwing flowers, roses mostly, that were falling at the soldiers' feet. But one of them landed on a soldier's tunic and somehow stuck there.

I saw him smile at that.

Like everyone else, I followed them round the town and up into the square.   The band played *God save the King* and then, with the Union Jack fluttering behind him, the first sergeant major I'd ever set eyes on got up on the steps of the cross, slipped his stick smartly under his arm, and spoke to us, his voice unlike any voice I'd heard before, rasping, commanding.

"I shan't beat about the bush, ladies and gentlemen," he began.   "I shan't tell you it's all tickety-boo out there in France - there's been too much of that nonsense already in my view.   I've been there.   I've seen it myself.   So I'll tell you straight.   It's no picnic.   It's hard slog, that's what it is, hard slog.   Only one question to ask yourself about this war.   Who would you rather see marching through your streets?   Us lot or the Huns?   Make up your minds.   Because mark my words, ladies and gentlemen, if we don't stop them out in France the Germans will be here, right here in Hatherleigh, right here on your doorstep."

"They'll come marching through here, burning your houses, killing your children, and yes, violating our women.   They've beaten brave little Belgium, swallowed her up in one gulp!   And they've taken a fair slice of France too.   I'm here to tell you that unless we beat them at their own game, they'll gobble us up as well."   His eyes raked over us.   "Well?   Do you want the Hun?   Do you?"

1.   The band plays 2 tunes during this extract.   What are these tunes?

2.   What were the children and the women doing as the band played and the soldiers marched?

3.   What are we told about the sergeant major's:-

   • appearance

   • voice.

4.   Now look closely at what the sergeant major says:
      How does he talk about the state of the war in France?

5.   In your own words what one question does he ask the crowd about the war?

6.   How does he describe what has happened in Belgium?

7.   What does his **eyes raked over us** mean?   Explain how this is a METAPHOR.

The world famous naturalist Gerald Durrell began his career looking after animals in Whipsnade zoo.   In his book *Beasts in My Belfry* he tells of some of his experiences.

On arriving in the morning the sunshine would be barely warm but it would give a brittle gold burnish to the leaves and grass and in its clear light you could see and hear the park coming awake.   Among the lurching shapes of the trees, droves of wallabies would squat in this quiet morning sun, plump bodies, fur covered with dew.   Clearly echoing across the paddocks, would come the strident "help...*help!*' of a peacock, dragging its coloured tail through the pine woods.   The zebras, as you passed, would throw up their heads and snort great fountains of steam at you and take nervous prancing steps in the wet grass. Turn onto the gravel paths that lead out of the section, and the polar bears would point quivering black noses at you from between the bars of their cage.   I would go down into the tiger pit where the iron gate would clatter, shaking a thousand vibrating echoes from the walls of the cement dungeons, and I would go inside to do the first jobs of the day.

The tigers would wake and greet me with pink – mouthed misty yawns, lying there in their beds of yellow, rustling straw.   Then they would stretch elegantly - long, curved - backed, stiff-tailed, nose-quivering stretches – before padding across their dens to peer at me through the barred doors.   In this pit lived two of our four tigers, Paul and Raneee, who were mother and son.   But Paul cherished no affection for his parent, so they had to sleep in separate dens and they were let out into the pit in turn.

Paul was the largest and fiercest of the tigers.

He had such perfection of movement and such a placid temperament that it was hard to believe that Ranee was really his mother. He moved silently and unhurriedly on his great pincushion paws; his mother moved just as silently but in a quick, nervous, jerky way that was unpleasantly suggestive of her ability to catch you unawares. I am quite sure that she spent most of her free time trying to evolve a successful method of killing us. She had a savage streak in her which showed in her unblinking green eyes. Paul would take meat from my hand with an air of quiet dignity and great gentleness; his mother would gulp at it ferociously and, if given the chance, take your hand as well. With Paul you got the impression that your hand, even if offered, would be considered an inferior object and, as such, ignored. It was a comforting thought, even if incorrect.

1. List the different types of animals Durrell mentions in this passage.

2. Which of the two tigers named is the more vicious?   Quote 2 phrases / sentences that prove this.

3. How did Paul the tiger eat the meat that was offered him?

4. The first paragraph creates a descriptive picture of the zoo coming to life in the morning.

Explain the following descriptive phrases and words:-

- golden burnish

- strident

- placid temperament

- an inferior object

- pincushion paws.

POETRY

Now that you've tried your hand at reading PROSE closely, let's try the same skills on POETRY.

Read the following poem carefully and answer the questions that follow.

What has happened to Lulu?

What has happened to Lulu, mother?

What has happened to Lu?

There's nothing in her bed but an old rag doll

And by its side a shoe.

Why is her window wide, mother,

The curtain flapping free,

And there's only a circle on the dusty shelf

Where her money-box used to be?

Why do you turn your head, mother,

And why do the tear-drops fall?

And why do you crumple that note on the fire

And say it is nothing at all?

I woke to voices late last night,

I heard an engine roar.

Why do you tell me the things I heard

Were a dream and nothing more?

I heard somebody cry, mother,

In anger or in pain,

But now I ask you why, mother,

You say it was a gust of rain.

Why do you wander about as though

You don't know what to do?

What has happened to Lulu, mother?

What has happened to Lu?

By Charles Causley

Often poems can be understood in a number of different ways. For instance, two people may have quite different ideas about each of the following:-

- who is the speaker of the poem, the one asking the questions
- who Lulu is
- what has happened to her
- what went on the previous night
- what is the note that the mother throws on the fire.

There are clues in the poem but these are details that can have more than one meaning. Think about what they COULD mean:-

- the rag doll
- one shoe
- why the mother is crying
- why the car engine **roared** the night before
- who was crying **in anger or in pain**
- why the mother is pretending that the noises were nothing but the rain.

1. Now that you have thought about all these details, write your account of what you think has most likely happened to Lulu, giving as much evidence from the poem as you can.

2. There are a number of questions in the poem - in fact almost every verse begins with question. What effect do all these questions have on you as you read the poem?

3. Do you think the poet should have solved the mystery for us and TOLD us what has happened - maybe by giving the mother's reply? Give your reasons.

Now look at William Blake's poem *The Lamb* in which the order of some of the lines has been changed. **Put the lines in the correct sequence.**

Little Lamb who made thee
Dost thou know who made thee
Gave thee life & bid thee feed.
Gave thee clothing of delight,
By the stream & o'er the mead;
Softest clothing wooly bright;
Gave thee such a tender voice,
Little Lamb who made thee
Dost thou know who made thee
Making all the vales rejoice!

Little Lamb I'll tell thee,
He is called by thy name,
Little Lamb I'll tell thee!
He became a little child:
For he calls himself a Lamb:
He is meek & he is mild,
I a child & thou a lamb,
Little Lamb God bless thee.
We are called by his name.
Little Lamb God bless thee.

DRAMA

Now we have had a look at PROSE and POETRY we can use the same skills for DRAMA.

You only have TWO things to consider here:-

- what the characters say
- the stage directions.

READ THE FOLLOWING EXTRACT FROM A STAGE PLAY AND ANSWER THE QUESTIONS.

SCENE: Seven o'clock on Friday night outside a chip shop. Faye is talking to her friend Josie who is eating chips. Marco and Raz from school come up to them.

MARCO: Yo girls! Who's gonna give me a chip then? (makes a grab at Josie's chips. She pulls them away angrily).

JOSIE: Get your own, you cheapskate.

RAZ: (in a mock polite way) Please lovely Josie, may I have a chip?

JOSIE: (laughing) Of course you may. (holds out carton to him. He takes one).

FAYE: I'm gonna go now, Jose. Mum's off to work in a bit and I said I'd mind Alysha.

MARCO: (obviously disappointed) Are you going now then? I'll treat you to some chips. it's not often I offer.

RAZ: I'd take him up on his offer if I was you. (slyly). He's been talking about you all night. About how great you were in that talent show at school.

MARCO: (embarrassed) No – I just said she was pretty good - and you were.

RAZ: Just as good as Rihanna he said.

JOSIE: (laughing) Stop stirring Raz and have another chip. Better still, go in and get some of your own while Marco walks Faye home.

FAYE: No, it's OK, there's no need (half heartedly). It's only a few minutes away.

MARCO: Yeah, come on, Josie's right.   It's Friday night, getting dark.
I'll go with you – and Raz can queue for the chips.

RAZ: You off anywhere special, Jose?

(She shakes her head).

RAZ: Come in here with me and when Marco gets back from his mission of mercy, we could go up to town and see what's happening there - just to hang out I mean.

JOSIE: (pretending to think carefully about it).   Yeah, OK then.   Might as well.   Can't stay out long though   Nine o'clock curfew tonight.   Dad's home for the weekend.   Special meal blah blah.

FAYE: Then why are you eating chips, Jose?   Or did you just want to come out and hang around here- in case you saw anyone interesting? (laughs).

MARCO: See you in a bit then.   C'mon Miss Rihanna.   Get in the queue, Raz, man!

JOSIE AND Raz watch them move away.

JOSIE: (laughing quietly) At last!   She never stops going on about him.   You did well.

RAZ: (kisses her lightly on the cheek.   She looks surprised but pleased) It wasn't all about getting THEM together, you know.

They smile shyly at each other and enter the chip shop.

1.   Why can't Faye stay out later with the others?

2.   What time does Josie have to be home by? Why?

3.   What are the signs that Marco really likes Faye:-

  • from the stage directions

  • from what he says?

4.   Do you think Faye really wants Marco to walk her home?   Give your evidence.

5.   How do we know that Raz is really interested in Josie?   Give your evidence.

6.   Do you think that Josie is interested in Raz?   Give your evidence.

SECTION B   NON-FICTION

Every time we read a menu, an article on the internet or a flyer advertising a forthcoming attraction we are reading non-fiction.   We use the same type of reading skills for this too - skimming, scanning and close reading and we need the same PEE technique as we used in **SECTION A** for close reading.

We are going to look at examples of the many types of NON-FICTION we can come across in our everyday lives.

In order to find out how non-fiction has an impact on us, we need to look at some of the techniques writers use in:-

- ARTICLES
- LEAFLETS
- WEBPAGES
- BLOGS
- ADVERTISEMENTS

FACT?.......OR OPINION?

Although we read non-fiction for FACT and INFORMATION, we are often presented with OPINION.

Newspapers often try to influence our thoughts and opinions.   So do web pages and advertisements, flyers and blogs.   Sometimes we don't even realize that we are being persuaded because the techniques are clever.

Over the page are some of the most commonly used techniques which help to persuade us.

1. HEADLINES

When talking about headlines, never say they are BIG and BOLD - that's obvious.

That's what headlines are!   Look at what they say and how they say it...

CAMERON DEFEATED IN COMMONS

It's pretty clear what these articles are going to be about.   But sometimes in the TABLOID newspapers, headlines try all kinds of ways to pull in the readers and make them stop turning the pages.

Sometimes there's a reference to POPULAR CULTURE/ PUBLIC FIGURES/ A WELL KNOWN SAYING.

Look at these headlines and try and identify which fairy tale they might refer to.

BEARS' BREKKIE BLAGGED BY BLONDE!

"GIANT NOT SO JOLLY" JOKES JACK

PINING PRICE SEEKS SWEETHEART TO FIT FOOTWEAR
WILY WOLF'S WICKEDNESS WIPED OUT BY WOOD CUTTER

Sometimes there is a joke or a play on words (PUN) which attracts our attention as in the headline below which is about a school where pupils are stopped from putting hands up in class to answer questions.

Thumbs down for hands up
School children in class ban

CELEBRITY BIG BLUBBER

RHYME is a useful technique to make headings leap out at the reader - and to add humour too. An article on losing weight, getting fit and becoming a more attractive young woman had the following catchy headline:

COUCH SLOUCH TO YUMMY MUMMY

*   **ALLITERATION**

is another favourite technique of the headline writers and the advertising copywriters e.g.

BRILLIANT BARNSLEY BATTLE ON

SAUCY SARAH STUNS SENIOR CITIZENS

*   Using eye catching PUNCTUATION can stop the newspaper browser in his tracks. EXCLAMATIONS, QUESTION MARKS all draw the reader in.

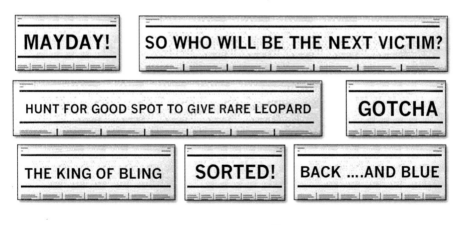

MAYDAY!

SO WHO WILL BE THE NEXT VICTIM?

HUNT FOR GOOD SPOT TO GIVE RARE LEOPARD

GOTCHA

THE KING OF BLING

SORTED!

BACK ....AND BLUE

SUBHEADINGS

These break up the text into smaller chunks so that we can take in what we read more easily.   They also act as SIGNPOSTS in the text so that we can find the bit that interests us most when we read.

2.   **LAYOUT**

You are often asked to examine this.   What does it actually mean?
You can consider the following:-

*   Is the piece in columns like a newspaper?
*   Does it have subheadings?
*   Does it use different size / style fonts to signal to the reader a different point or to add emphasis?
*   Is it written in paragraphs?   How long are these?   Why?   Do short paragraphs give impact to what is said?

REMEMBER

Paragraphs break up a text, give the eye and brain a short rest and allow us to take in what we are reading.   Consider:-

*   Are bullet points being used?
*   Have text boxes been used?
*   Do these contain brief summaries of the main points?

3.   **PICTURES / GRAPHICS / CARTOONS**

It's true that a picture can paint a thousand words when it comes to newspapers / magazines / leaflets.   When you examine any picture given in your piece, don't just say it's a picture of…. Think of the mood / image suggested in the picture over the page of the Queen at the opening ceremony for the 2012 Olympics.

Look closely at the picture and try to see why it was chosen.   If it's a holiday advertisement, does it show a beautiful beach and bright sunshine to sell the idea to you?   If it's for a theme park, does it show people smiling, having a good time?   If so, it's giving us the message that if we visit, we'll enjoy ourselves too.

4.   STATISTICS

Sometimes to make an argument more convincing, figures are quoted.   There are different ways to present figures and the writer will choose which way suits his/ her argument best.

Raw figures	**350,000**
Percentages	**35%**
Fractions	**1/3**
Ratios	**1 in 3**
Comparatively	**as tall as a double decker bus**

If we are told in an advertisement that 2 out of 3 people prefer a particular brand of tea, we might wonder why we ourselves don't buy it.   If we hear that 55% of young people at university have debts of over £10,000 we might be shocked. If we heard that 345,000 of pregnant women gave up smoking in pregnancy, we might feel the figure was encouraging BUT if we were told that less than 2% of pregnant women gave up, we might find this was disappointing, so the figure might not be presented in this way.

> **REMEMBER**
> There are ways to present statistics that will suit the message that the piece is trying to get across so always point this out.

5. **PERSONAL PRONOUNS**

To get us onside, the reader is often addressed directly using the personal pronoun YOU or

YOURS **e.g.** **YOU KNOW IT MAKES SENSE**

L'ORÉAL

Because You're Worth It

The advertisers often refer to themselves as **WE** or **US**, again to make us feel we can trust them.   This personal touch encourages confidence.

WE'RE IN IT TOGETHER

YOU KNOW IT MAKES SENSE

6. TRIPLING / THE RULE OF THREE

The magic number three works well with words. Three descriptive words in succession work better than two – or four.

There is something about the rhythm of triples which forces you to pay attention to the phrase and advertisers are very aware of this.

LOCATION, LOCATION, LOCATION

I CAME I SAW I CONQUERED

BLOOD SWEAT AND TEARS

7. SLOGANS

These are short snappy phrases that help a company to create confidence, humour and at the same time to reinforce the brand. Sometimes this will depend on a pun or imaginative spelling to make its impact....

A A DAY HELPS YOU WORK REST AND PLAY

NOKIA
Connecting People

"Melts in your mouth not in your hands"

8. LOGOS

These visual icons are easily identifiable, need no common language and give a sense of security of what to expect and make us feel that the product and what it stands for will be acceptable to us.

If we're lost in a maze of streets in Moscow, if we come across the golden arches of McDonalds, we immediately know:-

- what the food would be like
- it's not going to cost an arm and a leg
- we can point at the picture to identify it if our Russian isn't that good.

We can, of course, then go somewhere else because that's not what we came to Moscow for - but it's all quite reassuring.

i'm lovin' it™

9.   LANGUAGE

A writer's choice of words can heavily influence the way we feel about what we read.   EMOTIVE or LOADED LANGUAGE can manipulate our feelings so that we feel anger or pity, sympathy or disgust.   Advertising uses this type of language to persuade us to buy, but journalists - especially tabloid journalists - also load the language they use to get a point across

Look at these examples of emotive language and identify what we are being made to feel:-

- Innocent young puppies
- Drug crazed yobs
- Honest hard working parents
- Luxurious private yacht
- Succulent tender lamb
- Children tortured and maimed.

The choice of words is vital.

Words can be **neutral, negative** and **positive**.

Think of the words *slim* for example. Being slim is a positive idea, it's almost an obsession for some. But the word **SKINNY** conveys another idea - and it's not positive. Similarly to be **OBESE** is a negative word but someone who weighs just the same could be described as **PLUMP** in a kinder way.

Think about the words listed below and put them into three columns headed **NEGATIVE**, **POSTIVE** and **NEUTRAL**.

juicy	slimy	succulent	
compassionate	kind	gullible	
strong	obstinate	determined	pigheaded
gentle	weak	sensitive	
good	virtuous	goody - goody	
sunny	scorching	blistering	radiant
brave	valiant	ruthless	fearless
clever	intelligent	knowledgeable	bright
irresponsible	carefree	chilled	thoughtless
colourful	garish	eye-catching	vibrant

10. IMPERATIVES

These words tell us to DO something and advertisers love them:-

* **Stroll** *around the town and visit the local markets*

* **Buy** *one of these and your life will never be the same .*

IMPERATIVES are the bossy form of a verb.   You will find them in **DIRECTIONS** too e.g.

Take a left and continue along for another hundred yards then follow the road to the bridge.

You also find them in instruction manuals like cookery books e.g.

Now cream the butter together with the sugar.

11. PUNCTUATION

QUESTIONS draw the reader in. They involve you in what you are reading:

WHAT MAKES A GREAT FAMILY HOLIDAY?

The reader has probably some ideas of his / her own about that - sunshine, beaches, fun, great food - so we're attracted to the piece.

EXCLAMATION MARKS can often be used and overused to suggest surprise, shock, horror.   The message is **look at what I'm saying, take notice and react**. To use more than one is lazy and lessens the effect.

a.   NEWSPAPER ARTICLES

Now look at the following article and see how many of these techniques you can spot.

Children 'more likely to own a mobile phone than a book'

Children as young as seven are more likely to own a mobile phone than a book,

i

figures show, fuelling fears over a decline in reading.

Almost 9 in 10 pupils now have a mobile compared with fewer than three-quarters who have their own books in the home, it was disclosed.

The study by the National Literacy Trust suggested a link between regular access to books outside school and high test scores.

According to figures, some 80 percent of children with better than expected reading skills had their own books, compared with just 58 percent who were below the level expected for their age group.

The disclosure follows the publication of a study found that found keeping just 20 books in the home could boost children's chances of doing well at school.

Jonathan Douglas, National Literacy Trust director, said: "Our research illustrates the clear link with literacy resources at home and a child's reading ability, as well the vital importance of family encouragement."

"By ensuring children have access to reading materials in the home and by encouraging children to love reading, families can help them to do well at school and to enjoy opportunities throughout their life."

As part of the latest study, the trust surveyed more than 17,000 schoolchildren aged seven to sixteen.

It found that 85.5 percent of pupils had their own mobile phone, compared with 72.6 percent who had their own books. Among children in Key Stage 2 – aged seven to eleven – 79.1 percent had a mobile compared with 72.7 percent who had access to books.

The research comes as the trust launches a new campaign - Tell Me a Story - which aims to raise awareness of the need for families to support children's literacy.

To launch the campaign, the trust is calling on families to spend 10 minutes reading with children as part of Family Week Story Time on June 2.

There is also ample evidence that parents who promote reading as a valuable and worthwhile activity have children who are motivated to read for pleasure.

SECTION B – Non-Fiction

NEWSPAPER ARTICLES

Books Vs. Mobiles / Texting

1. Who conducted the study on books and mobile phones?
2. How many books in the home can make a difference to a pupil's performance in school?
3. What is the difference in the percentage of pupils who have a mobile phone and those who had their own books?
4. What is the new campaign called which will show the need to support children's literacy?

UK Text Messaging Teens Use Only 800 Words a Day **ii**

A generation of teenagers who communicate via the Internet and by text messages are risking unemployment because their daily vocabulary consists of just 800 words, the UK's new children's communication expert has warned. Although, according to recent surveys, they know an average of 40,000 words, they tend to favour a "teenspeak" used in text messages, on social networking sites like Facebook and MySpace and in internet chat rooms like MSN.

TESCO One poll, commissioned by Tesco, revealed that while children had the vocabulary to be articulate, the top 20 words they used including "yeah", "no" and "but", accounted for about a third of all the words they used.

According to Jean Gross, England's first Communication Champion for Children who started in the post this month, the lack of range will impact negatively on their chances of getting a job.

"Teenagers are spending more time communicating through electronic media and text messaging, which is short and brief," she told The Sunday Times. "We need to help today's teenagers understand the difference between their textspeak and the formal language they need to succeed in life · 800 words will not get you a job."

1.   Why according to Jean Gross has teenagers' vocabulary shrunk to about 800 words?

2.   What does **will impact negatively** on their chances of getting a job mean?

3.   Give 3 examples of TEXTSPEAK from your own experience then give the FORMAL meaning of those expressions.

4.   This is an example of a very famous couple of lines written in TEXTSPEAK.   Write the lines in the language they were originally written in.

> "2 b, r nt 2 b dat iz d Q wthr ts noblr n d mnd 2 sufr d slngs & arowz of outrAjs fortn r 2 tAk armz agnst a C f trblz, & by

b.   WEB ARTICLES

Read the following web article and answer the questions that follow

---

Holidays in Wales

What makes a great UK family holiday?

Family Friendly

All families are different, but we believe that there are some basic requirements for a good family holiday.   Most family breaks run smoothly when the children are entertained and occupied - child friendly days out make for happier kids and parents.   Here's what we think.....

- Make it an experience - the style of family holiday can be an adventure in itself.   Staying on a farm, camping in the woods or right by the sea all offer a great alternative for families looking for a 'different' holiday experience.

- Holiday on a budget - the credit crunch has meant that many families are on the look out for budget UK holidays.   We have some budget break ideas coupled with free day out suggestions that may help.

- Remove the stress - there are the obvious advantages of holidaying in the UK (or

---

the Staycation as it's increasingly being referred to), no airport delays, strikes, parking fee lost baggage and related hassle. From this perspective Wales is very accessible, being a little over two hours from most of the big UK cities.

Activities and Outdoor Adventure

Gentle family walks

Want to give your family some fresh air and stretch their legs? Then take them on a walk along the coast, under waterfalls, through rolling trees or even up a mountain.

Here are a few ideas:-

- Walk the Pembrokeshire Coastal Path or at least part
- Hike through Snowdonia National Park
- Nature trails around Lake Vyrnwy
- Walk the gentle and historic Usk Valley route
- Walk with the wildlife in the Brecon Beacons National Park.

Take the kids to stay on a farm

Going on a farm holiday is fun. The kids can feed the animals and see how they live. You may even be able to collect your eggs for breakfast. You get to stay in the beautiful Welsh countryside in a rustic farm house with wonderful views. Wales has a range of farm stays to suit families, go self-catering or take the B&B option.

The first place to check for a farmstay is Farm Stay Wales, here are some examples of the range of farmstays available:-

- Tyddyn-du-Farm (Porthmadag)

- Nannerth Country Holidays (Wye Valley)

- Parc-le- breos (Gower)

- Pentretai Farm (Cardiff/Newport)

- Knock Farm (Pembrokeshire).

Traffic free cycling & mountain biking

Wales has 331 miles of traffic - free rides, perfect for children. Take them on a day out to cycle one of Wales' forest trails or coastal paths. We even have trails in our capital city.

First things first, you should visit our cycling and mountain biking websites. For more details cycling breaks there is more to be found on Sustrans.

The cycling and mountain bike websites will show all routes available but here are a few to get you started:-

- Cycle along Swansea's seafront

- Gently introduce yourself to mountain biking at Coed y Brenin's Yr Afon forest trail

- Cycle the beautiful Elan Valley alongside reservoirs
- The Celtic Trail offers traffic free cycling along the Millennium Coastal path
- Find more family friendly rides in Wales.

Family Friendly Beaches

Beaches are always a firm family favourite...

- Find your perfect beach
- Blue Flag beaches in Wales
- Keep Wales Tidy Coastal Awards

Take the Kids Surfing

A day out surfing can be loads of fun for all the whole family. Wales has some great areas for surfing like the Gower Peninsular, closely followed by much of the Welsh coastline.   If you'd prefer not to swallow all that sea water after a wipe-out there's an indoor surf centre in Swansea too.

Here are some awesome places for visting as well:-

- LC2's BoardRider (Swansea)
- Gower Surf School (Gower).

1.   Look closely at the pictures in this website.   Explain carefully how they link with the headings and how they might persuade people to take a holiday in Wales.

2.   How do the bullet points in each section help the reader to find out more information?

4.   Find an example of a question in the advertisement.

5.   Now choose 5 words / phrases from the website that show HOW the site tries to influence holidaymakers to visit Wales and explain why they are persuasive.

Opening 2012 ceremony watched by 27 million people in the UK

Almost 27 million people in the UK watched the London opening ceremony.

That makes it the 13th most watched programme in British TV history.

It was also the most watched Olympic opening ceremony in the UK with five times more people watching the show than the ceremony in Beijing in 2008.

The biggest audience ever in the UK for a single programme was way back in 1986 when a mega 30.5 million people tuned into a special episode of EastEnders on Christmas day.

Inside the stadium 65,000 lucky ticket holders got to see the ceremony up close.

The show was rehearsed more than 200 times before the big day.

Each of the 7,500 volunteers had to spend around 150 hours practising in the run up to the show.

1.   Does this article give us FACT OR OPINION?
2.   How does it back up its facts?
     the most watched opening ceremony.
4.   Approximately how many Britons watched the opening ceremony in Beijing in 2008?
5.   What is the record figure for the highest recorded viewing audience for a TV programme in the UK?   What programme was this?
7.   Approximately how many days worth of practice did the volunteers put in for the opening ceremony?

iii

Online time 'is good for teens'

By Maggie Shiels

Technology reporter, BBC News, Silicon Valley

Hanging out online develops core social skills, the report said. Surfing the internet, playing games and hanging out on social networks are important for teen development, a large study of online use has revealed.

The report contradicts the **stereotypical** view held by many parents and teachers that such activity is a waste of time.

More than 800 teenagers and parents took part in the three-year US project.

"They are learning the technological skills and literacy needed for the **contemporary** world," said the report's author, Dr Mimi Ito.

"They are learning how to communicate online, craft a public identity, create a home page, post links.

"All these things were regarded as **sophisticated** 10 years ago but young people today take them for granted," Dr Ito told the BBC.

Dr Ito said that connecting online with friends via social networks such as MySpace and Facebook was where teens now "hang out", compared to the usual public places like shopping malls, the street and parks.

DIGITAL GAP

The researchers discovered a digital divide between those who have **access** to the web and those who do not.

"The quality of access is what matters for some kids who have to just rely on the library and school to go online. It is often limited, has blocks put on access to certain sites and is only available when these **institutions** are open," said Dr Ito.

SECTION B – Non-Fiction

REVIEW

Toy Story 3

1. In which country was this study carried out?

2. Where according to Dr Ito do many teenagers now 'hang out'?

3. Not all teenagers have equal opportunity in using the web. What does she say are the two different groups of teenagers?

4. What does the passage say are the disadvantages of only having access to public computers?

5. What do the words and phrases in bold mean?

6. Why are Dr Ito's actual words quoted so frequently in the article?

c. REVIEWS

i

Sing and dance ... stars Buzz and Jessie......Light years ahead
By ALEX ZANE
PIXAR, the studio that started the computer animation revolution, return to the franchise that began it all. And Toy Story 3 shows why they remain the masters of the genre.

This is an almost flawless example of a movie that will keep pretty much any person of any age enthralled and entertained.

It's 15 years since the original Toy Story and the audience that first embraced Woody the cowboy (Tom Hanks), Buzz Lightyear (Tim Allen) and the rest of the gang so warmly has grown up a lot.

Plastic fantastic ... Jodie Benson and Michael Keaton provide the voices for Barbie and Ken. But fear not. Pixar, as usual, are one step ahead and have created a film that deals with adult themes such as unemployment, retirement and even the purpose of existence.

Yet it still appeals to the youngsters with a classic battle of good versus evil.

Friends reunited ... the gang are back but fighting for survival
Opening with an explosive sequence that outdoes any of the summer's action offerings — bridges detonate, trains plummet and monkeys attack — we suddenly find ourselves at the point where the toys' owner Andy (John Morris) is a teenager heading off to college.

Worrying about their future and whether they'll be thrown away or sent to live out their lives in the attic, the toys decide to band together and face their fate.

That's apart from the plastic military men who rightly observe, as they parachute out of the window, that "when the trash bags come out, us army guys are the first to go".
An unfortunate mistake sees the other toys donated to a local daycare centre which, although on the surface seems a wonderful new home, turns out to harbour some dark secrets, as well as this film's major new cast members.

The best of this bunch is Ken (Michael Keaton) who, alongside Barbie (Jodie Benson), brings the exact voice to their decades-long relationship — the one we've always imagined they've had but could never actually hear.

There's also Big Baby, a child's doll who will surely set back sales of plastic infants by thousands.

The tear - inducing finale — I challenge you not to at least well up — is a superb and emotional end to a series that will continue to be watched and adored by new generations for years to come. VERDICT: Five out of five

1.   Explain the play on words in the heading to the review.

2.   What does ***masters of the genre*** mean?

3.   What does ***almost flawless examples*** mean?

4.   Quote the phrase/sentence that tells us that way the film is likely to appeal to adults as well as children.

5.   Three new cast members are mentioned.   Who are they?

6.   What does ***tear inducing finale*** mean?

7.   Choose 3 words/phrases from the review that show clearly that the reviewer really likes the film.

Telly gold we won't forget: Why the Olympic Games opening ceremony was the greatest show on TV... EVER

With ratings soaring to an astonishing 26.9 million, our hero Danny Boyle treated us to three hours and 45 minutes of pure TV gold.

Jamie Squire   **ii**
Sure, it was the greatest show on Earth. But London's breathtaking opening ceremony was also the greatest show on - television.   Ever.

With ratings soaring to an astonishing 26.9 million, our hero Danny Boyle treated us to three hours and 45 minutes of pure TV gold.
We have never seen anything like it...

The Queen co-starring with James Bond? Give that monarch a Bafta!
Beaming David Beckham's well - deserved moment of glory in a speed boat which carried the Olympic torch on the penultimate stage of its 8,000-mile journey. He was so proud to be British. And so were we.

Olympian colossus Sir Steve Redgrave running into the packed stadium. The awesome lighting of the flame. The coming together of those burning copper petals. The blazing Olympic rings. The fabulous fireworks. All of it... just jaw-dropping.

It was a milestone in broadcasting history.   Four years ago, Beijing's lavish ceremony was wonderful. But it was a stage show at which they pointed the cameras.

London's was a stunning television programme. Seamlessly cutting away to Her Majesty's hilarious parachute jump and to Mr Bean's funny Chariots of Fire fantasy.

As one surprise followed another, this epic spectacle was the best of British... There was comedy, there was drama, there was music, there was laugh-out-loud barminess.   After all, we are renowned as a nation of eccentrics.

Where else would you hear, "Ladies and Gentleman... please welcome Mike Oldfield and the staff of the National Health Service"?

Where else would you hear the Arctic Monkeys playing Come Together while hundreds of cyclists rode around in luminous wings?

Where else would the Queen and the Duke of Edinburgh have to grin and bear it as the Sex Pistols' punk classic Pretty Vacant was blasted out at top volume?

1. How long does the review say the programme lasted?

2. Did David Beckham carry the torch on the last stage of its journey?   Quote the word that tells us.

3. What does the expression **grin and bear it** mean?

4. Why do you think the review uses the words **we** and **our** in this article?

5. What is the effect of using the words:-

   - awesome
   - stunning
   - hilarious
   - fabulous
   - moment of glory
   - luminous.

6. Why did the last three sentences on the review begin with **why else**?

d. LEAFLET / BROCHURE

SKIM AND SCAN the following 2 pieces for the information needed to answer the questions.

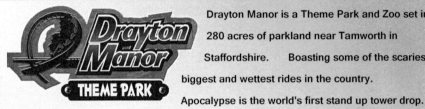

Drayton Manor is a Theme Park and Zoo set in 280 acres of parkland near Tamworth in Staffordshire.   Boasting some of the scariest, biggest and wettest rides in the country.

Apocalypse is the world's first stand up tower drop.

Shockwave is Europe's only stand up rollercoaster.   Stormforce 10 is 'the best water rides in the country' (Daily Express) and G-Force terrifies thrill seekers with speeds of up to 70kph at 4.3 G's, all while hanging from your hip.   Not for the lighthearted!

For youngsters there are age appropriate rides, shows and entertainment.   The *recently opened Thomas Land is a must for all Thomas the tank engine fans* with 12 themed rides, indoor play area and merchandise shop.

For a quieter experience, the Zoo is home to over a hundred species including big cats, reptiles, monkeys, owls, eagles, parrots - plus an *exotic creature reserve*.

Height restrictions and health restrictions apply to some rides and details of these can be found on the website.

Opening Times

Open from 20th March to 31st October 2011.

Gates open at 9.30am.

Rides from 10.30am until 5.00pm (please note that ride queues may close earlier).

The park is closed on 20th, 21st, 27th & 28th September 2010 and 4th, 5th, 11th, 12th, 18th & 19th October 2011 (the Zoo will be open).

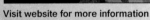

Visit website for more information

Ticket Prices

Adult - £28.00

Child (4-11) - £24.00

Disabled - £18.00

Under 4yrs – Free

1. Which county in England is Drayton Manor in?
2. What is the name of Europe's only stand up rollercoaster?
3. How much does it cost for a ticket for a four year old child?
4. How much would it cost for the following family to visit Drayton Manor?
   2 children, 4 adults, one of whom is in a wheelchair.
5. What does the **recently opened Thomas Land is a must for all Thomas the tank engine fans** mean?
6. What is an *exotic creature* reserve?